Psalm One for Women on the Run

Psalm One for Women on the Run

Valerie Cullers

Psalm One for Women on the Run

© Valerie Cullers 2018

All rights reserved. Without limiting the rights under
copyright reserved above, no part of this publication may
be reproduced, stored in a retrieval system, or transmitted,
in any form or by any means (electronic, mechanical,
photocopying, recording or otherwise), without the prior
written permission of the copyright owner of this book.

Published by
Lighthouse Christian Publishing
SAN 257-4330
5531 Dufferin Drive
Savage, Minnesota, 55378
United States of America

www.lighthousechristianpublishing.com

Scripture quotations marked (NIV) are taken from the Holy Bible, New International Version®, NIV®, Copyright ©1973, 1978, 1984, 2011 by Biblica, Inc.™ Used by permission of Zondervan. All rights reserved worldwide www.zondervan.com. The "NIV" and New International Version" are trademarks registered in the United States Patent Trademark Office by Biblica, Inc.™

PREFACE

How busy is your life? Are you running most of the day? Do you want to spend time in God's word daily, but you just can't find the time? Well, this Bible Study is written with you in mind.

Every scripture verse that you need to look up will be in the lesson for you. You can put this booklet in your purse, diaper bag, or your briefcase. You can take it out when you have a few free minutes and read part of the lesson and answer the questions. I have tried to make this as user friendly as possible. I want you, the reader, to enjoy the beauty of God's word and know that it applies to you, wherever you find yourself.

So please, come along with me and we'll discover some great truths written in the scripture. You will find it's wisdom relevant and applicable to your life. I hope you will learn to love it as much as I do.

INTRODUCTION

Some women have a life verse. They can quote it for you at the drop of a hat. They will tell you it is the verse that has meant the most to them throughout their life as a believer. For me, there are many verses that have spoken to me at different times and in different situations. The verses I remember the most from the early days when I first became a Christian are the ones in Psalm One.

I first heard a Bible college student give a sermon on this psalm and from then on I memorized it, meditated on it, and began to try to understand what it truly meant. Over the years, I have seen the lessons of this psalm played out in many different situations. The Bible really is true and you will see that the advice it gives is priceless. The wisdom it offers is invaluable, no matter what situation you find yourself in. It doesn't matter if you are a stay at home mom, the head of a large corporation, or serving in our military in some faraway place.

Psalm One was written over two millennia ago, but its message is timeless. Biblical scholars do not know who wrote this Psalm. It may have been written by King David, it may not have been. In order to put it in a historical context, I am taking some creative license and suggesting its authorship might be attributed to David. Before each lesson, there is a fictional narrative showing how this Psalm may have been given to him by the Holy Spirit. I have placed him in his hometown of Bethlehem. For our purposes, he is a young teenager, still tending the sheep of his father, Jesse.

Wherever you live in this modern world, and whatever situation you find yourself in; my hope is that you take two very important truths with you from this study. First, spending time in God's word and applying its truths will lead you into a blessed and fruitful life. Second, you can trust God with your ultimate destiny because you have made Him and his word the ultimate priority of your life. So, let's get started. I can hardly wait for you to discover some of the treasures that are in this psalm!

Psalm One

1 Blessed is the man who does not walk in the counsel of the wicked or stand in the way of sinners or sit in the seat of mockers.

2 But his delight is in the law of the LORD, and on his law he meditates day and night.

3 He is like a tree planted by streams of water, which yields its fruit in season and whose leaf does not wither. Whatever he does prospers.

4 Not so the wicked! They are like chaff that the wind blows away.

5 Therefore the wicked will not stand in the judgment, nor sinners in the assembly of the righteous.

6 For the LORD watches over the way of the righteous, but the way of the wicked will perish.

(NIV)

The Psalmist's Tale

It was the cool of the morning, the time of day that David loved the most. The sun had been above the horizon for about an hour, not long enough to add any heat to the day. There was a slight breeze, just enough to dry any perspiration off of him as he walked up the hill. The sheep were quietly grazing on the lush green grass, still wet with the morning dew.

He loved taking care of his father's sheep. His brothers mocked him at times, being the youngest and smallest, therefore having to do this job that no one wanted. He couldn't tell them how much he loved being out of doors and away from the noises of the household. Who could stand the incessant talking of his mother and sisters, and the arguing of his brothers, as they postured for supremacy in the family?

No, this was the life for him. Out in the fields each day, with no one telling him what to do. Here, he could be his own boss, and the boss of these sheep. Taking care of them gave him plenty to do. He needed to keep a watchful eye on each of the animals. There was always the threat of a hungry predator, waiting to snatch one of the lambs away from its mother's care. They weren't the smartest of animals, and at times they would wander off if you didn't watch them carefully.

And when it was quiet, and it usually was, he could enjoy the beauty of his surroundings. He could scarcely take it all in, the azure sky, the sea of verdant grass, and the leaves as they rustled with every breath of wind. He even loved the smell of the outdoors, especially the moist earth with all its potential for growth. He had the heart of a poet, but dared not show this side of himself to his brothers. They knew he was a musician, and only tolerated his playing because it seemed to help his mother when she wasn't feeling well.

What he liked most about his job, though, was the way he felt when he was out here by himself. He didn't feel alone in the hills. He felt closer to God in this unspoiled environment. He would think about the words his father had taught him from the law, God's sacred law.

And since Samuel the prophet had anointed him, he could really say he felt God's presence. Of course he didn't share it with anyone for fear of more verbal reprisals. He could hear God whisper in his spirit. He heard words and he couldn't forget them. He would put them to music and sing them to the Lord during the day and he would think about what they meant during the night:

"Blessed is the man who does not walk in the counsel of the wicked or stand in the way of sinners or sit in the seat of mockers."

Oh yes, he wanted to be blessed. He felt he already was more blessed than anyone he knew. Hadn't he been anointed by the prophet? Even though only his family knew it, it was still wonderful to him. To think that someday God would have a special job for him to do! What had happened seemed like a dream to him now, but he knew that somehow, someway, God would bring it to pass when he was older.

He knew he didn't want to take counsel from wicked men. There were plenty of them around, just waiting to make another convert to their crooked philosophy. He didn't want to hang around with them either. He had seen what some of the men did who wanted to be part of that group. He had seen the cheating in the market place, the taking advantage of those less fortunate than they, and it made him angry. How dare they? Didn't they know that someday, they would have to account for their actions?

They didn't behave that way, though. They just made fun of anyone who made less than they did because they were honest. After all, if you could lie and make a little more money, what was wrong with that? That was just shrewd business practices. Hah! What a lie!

Valerie Cullers

LESSON ONE

**"Blessed is the man who does not walk in the counsel of the wicked
or stand in the way of sinners or sit in the seat of mockers."
(Psalm 1: 1)**

Psalm One is a beautiful psalm of comparisons and contrasts. It may have been written by David, the Shepherd-King of Israel. He lived almost three thousand years ago,[1] but what he wrote is still relevant to us today. David, through the inspiration of the Holy Spirit, wrote almost half of the psalms in the Old Testament He was a poet and musician, and many of his psalms were set to music. He had a real love for the word of God and he stated it many times in the psalms he wrote. Let's take a look at this first one.

I.   **"Blessed is the man"**

David knew what the word blessed meant. In Hebrew the word blessed is defined as "blessed, happy."[2] We don't need anyone to tell us what happy is, that we understand,

---

[1] David (king). Encarta. Microsoft Corporation. 1993-2002.
[2] Strong, James, <u>Strong's Exhaustive Concordance of the Bible</u>. A Concise Dictionary Of The Words in The Hebrew Bible. Hendrickson Publishers.18.

but what about blessed ? One definition for blessed in my dictionary is "enjoying happiness; fortunate."[3] What is your definition of blessed? Is it material possessions, a happy marriage or children? Would the picture include a good job, status of some sort or fulfillment in another area of life? Let's see how the Bible defines the blessed person.

1. "Blessed are those who have learned to acclaim you, who walk in the light of your presence, O LORD." (Psalm 89:15)

"Blessed is the man who finds wisdom, the man who gains understanding, for she is more profitable than silver and yields better returns than gold." (Proverbs 3:13)

What are some of the characteristics of the blessed woman? After reading the above scriptures, describe her in your own words.

2. Are you blessed? Do you feel that God's blessing is on your life? Why or why not?

II. "Who does not walk in the counsel of the wicked"

In David's day, just as in today's society, there were many kinds of people. There were those who followed the Lord. You could usually pick them out because of their lifestyle. They were referred to as righteous or godly people. There were those who were definitely not doing the right thing. Again, you could pick these people out by their lifestyle. Those who were living a lifestyle that was immoral were called wicked or ungodly. The word, wicked as it is used here means morally wrong in the Hebrew.[4]

---

[3] The American Heritage Dictionary, Second College Edition. Boston, MA: Houghton Mifflin Company, 1976. 187.
[4] Strong, James, Strong's Exhaustive Concordance of the Bible. A Concise Dictionary Of The Words In The Hebrew Bible. Hendrickson Publishers.111.

Valerie Cullers

Psalm One tells us that the blessed or happy woman does not do three things. First, the blessed or happy woman does not walk in the counsel of the wicked. In the Bible, our walk is usually synonymous with our lifestyle. So the blessed woman is not living her life based on the advice she was given by someone who is living a life that is morally wrong.

At first glance, we think, "Gee, I don't do that! I don't even want to do that!" But then we have to ask ourselves, do we? Do we take counsel from the wicked without even knowing we are doing so? Who are we listening to and taking counsel from?

Who are the people you go to for help or advice? At their core, what are their spiritual values? What about the way they are living? Do they give you godly counsel or do they give you advice that is worldly or different from what the word of God teaches?

What about the advice we hear on the television talk shows? Some of the people on those shows probably would fall into this category. Some of them seem good, they are beautiful and appear to be rich. Their lives look so full. Surely, they must know what they are talking about. But do we even know what their core beliefs and lifestyles are?

Many people on these shows seem to have a buffet kind of philosophy. They may take some of their ideas from the Bible, some from eastern religions, some from the New Age movement, or some from other sources. You can't really put it into any one category. It might sound pretty good, but what they are saying may not really line up with the Bible. So ask yourself, how much of it you are taking in? Are you following it without even knowing you are doing so?

3. "The plans of the righteous are just, but the advice of the wicked is deceitful." (Proverbs 12: 5) Have you found the advice of the wicked to be deceitful? Can you name a time when

you were given the wrong advice and followed it?

4. "For the wisdom of this world is foolishness in God's sight. As it is written, "He catches the wise in their craftiness," and again, "The Lord knows that the thoughts of the wise are futile." (1 Corinthians 3:19)

If the wisdom of this world is foolishness in God's sight, how do you look at it? Are you constantly going to worldly sources for your counsel? Why or why not?

III. **"Or stand in the way of sinners."**

The second thing we should not do is stand in the way of sinners. We are starting to see a progression here. Walking has now become standing, and someone has gone from taking counsel from the wicked to standing around with sinners.

Is there a difference in what the Bible calls a wicked person and a sinner? In the Hebrew, the word sinner means "a criminal or one accounted guilty."[5] Do you know people who are constantly getting into trouble for what they do? These are the people we don't want to hang around, otherwise they may lead us into trouble.

What would this picture look like? We might think of a young person walking home from school with the wrong crowd. They all stop to congregate and talk about what they are going to do that afternoon. Should she stop or keep going? Our common sense would tell us that this person should keep going. We know that if she stands around with those who are always getting into trouble, she will be doing the same things they do.

---

[5] Strong,< James, <u>Strong's Exhaustive Concordance of the Bible</u>. Hendrickson Publishers. (A Concise Dictionary of the words in the Hebrew Bible). 38

Not only will she be doing the same things, but she will eventually suffer the same consequences they do.

Has this ever happened to you? Have you ever been with a group of people and you got sucked into what they were doing? Later, when you thought about what you did, do you wish you would have just kept going?

I know that in my life I have experienced this. One night after a football game in high school, my boyfriend and I were walking home. Some of his friends from school asked us if we would like a ride home. After we got in the car, they explained that they had some eggs and were going to egg the other team's bus. Really, what could be the harm in that? We thought it sounded fun, and so we didn't ask them to take us home first. We all got out of the car and had our eggs in hand. As the bus started over a bridge, we threw the eggs at it. It continued on, and we just laughed. As we went down to Main Street to enjoy our triumph, a police car stopped and asked us about the incident. Apparently, someone had gotten the car's license number. We were taken to the police station and questioned about the incident. Our parents were called and you can bet I wished I had never gotten into that car that night.

This verse is telling us that if we want to be happy and blessed, we should avoid doing this sort of thing. We want to be consciously thinking about what we are doing and who we are doing it with. It warns us to not be naïve so we won't foolishly end up in places doing things we shouldn't do. Then, we will not have to suffer the consequences of our wrong behavior.

5. "Do not set foot on the path of the wicked or walk in the way of evil men. Avoid it, do not travel on it; turn from it and go on your way. For they cannot sleep till they do evil; they are robbed of slumber till they make someone fall." (Proverbs 4:14-16)

Obviously, the path of the wicked is a negative path. In these verses, what happens to those who walk on it? What do they do to others?

Have you or are you currently walking on it? Explain.

6. "The path of the righteous is like the first gleam of dawn, shining ever brighter till the full light of day. But the way of the wicked is like deep darkness; they do not know what makes them stumble." (Proverbs 4:18-19)

These two verses contrast paths to walk on. Which do you want to walk on and why?

IV.   "Or sit in the seat of mockers."

We can see the progression here. So far, this verse has told us not to walk in bad counsel, stand with those who do wrong and finally not to sit where they sit. Have you ever hung out with the wrong crowd? If you have, you know that they save a place for you. It could be in the cafeteria, lounge or a break room. You are part of this crowd and you feel safe. But you know what they do to others. They may gossip, and tear down those that won't go along with them and do what they do. What are these people called?

    These people are "mockers." Without any help from the Hebrew, we know who mockers are. They are the ones who make fun of anyone who is trying to do good or different things than what they do. The word in Hebrew means "have in derision, mocker, scorn."[6]

When I was in high school, I was part of a group that made fun of others. It felt safe to be with them, because they weren't making fun of me. It didn't make me feel good, however. When I left the lunchroom, I felt bad inside. I knew I had done something wrong and had hurt others. As I got older, I didn't want to be part of that group, even if it meant that they would be making fun of me.

People are afraid of mockers because they have a lot of verbal power. The only way to have power over them is to live a godly life. Only God can give us the strength and power to live above this crowd and not be brought down by them. Don't be fooled by what you see; mockers are not happy people. If they were, they wouldn'tt have to make fun of people who are different than they are.

7. "Drive out the mocker, and out goes strife; quarrels and insults are ended." (Proverbs 22:10)

Do you live and work around mockers? How does this scripture say they affect the atmosphere around them?

Sometimes, we cannot drive out a mocker, but what can you do to avoid being around one?

8. "If you are wise, your wisdom will reward you; if you are a mocker, you alone will suffer." (Proverbs 9:12)

Again we see two different lifestyles. What are the consequences of each?

---

[6] Strong, James, Strong's Exhaustive Concordance Of The Bible. Hendrickson Publishers.(A Concise Dictionary of the Words in the Hebrew Bible). 59.

Describe the lifestyle you are living and what you are experiencing now.

In conclusion, if we want to be happy and blessed, let us not walk in the counsel of the wicked, stand in the way of sinners, or sit in the seat of mockers. This verse talks about what we don't want to do. In the next lesson, we will find out what we are to do so that we will be happy and blessed.

The Psalmist's Tale

It had been an unusually warm day for the beginning of spring. The sun was about to set, and a cool breeze was beginning to blow across the land. David decided to keep the sheep out a few nights. He had gone far enough into the hills that he didn't want to return home. He had enough food to last for a few days, and there were several streams that he and the sheep could drink from. There was a cave at the end of the valley that was perfect to keep the sheep in at night. The sheep were protected there and all he had to do was watch the front. He would build a fire and play his harp this evening. The noise and light would serve to alert any would-be intruder that the sheep were not alone.

He felt warm by the fire now. It's funny how it could be so hot during the day, and then get so cold once the sun set. That's how it was in Israel; it was a land of contrasts. It created a strong, rugged people, who could adapt to what it afforded. He loved it, and enjoyed spending his nights outdoors.

He picked up his harp to play one of the songs he had heard the Levites sing. There were so many that spoke of the greatness of God and how he had delivered them from their enemies. There were many that just praised God and thanked him for his creation. As David looked up in the sky, he felt awestruck by the giant expanse. It made him feel tiny on the earth. But he knew God could still see him and hear his voice.

When he finished playing, he sat and meditated on the words his father had taught him from the law. Surely one had to be careful to do all that the Lord required of his people. The only way to do that was to think about what it said and try to keep it in mind at all times.

This wasn't a burden to him, though. The laws that God had given Moses made sense and helped him in every area of his life. He knew the laws had been given to make them into a kind and just people. They were supposed to be an example to others of the goodness of God.

What he loved the most though, was the real heart of the law; the love that God had for his people and the love he wanted in return. Hadn't God said that he was a faithful God and his love extended to a thousand generations to those that kept his commandments? David knew that it was really about a love relationship with the Lord and not just following all of the commands. He wanted to love the Lord with all of his heart, soul and mind. That kind of love would help him keep the commands.

One way to show his love was to sing his songs to the Lord. He knew that it pleased him, and he felt like the Lord was giving him the words and the melody. Right now, the next line was coming to the song that he had begun earlier in the day:

"But his delight is in the law of the LORD, and on his law he meditates day and night." He would smooth the music out to fit the words. He would work on it this evening as he kept watch over the sheep. He knew it would be a good song when it was finished, one that would really please the Lord.

LESSON TWO

**"But his delight is in the law of the Lord, and on his law he meditates day and night."
(Psalm 1:2)**

Many times in the psalms, the Psalmist writes about the law of the Lord and how much he delights in it. He uses words like love to describe how he feels about God's law. Ordinarily, you and I don't necessarily think in those terms as we think about God's laws. Let's look at this second verse to see if we can discover the secret of the blessed woman and see how she uses her mind.

I.   **"But his delight"**

Delight, what a word! Both my English dictionary and Hebrew dictionary say that this word carries a sense of pleasure. The blessed woman is getting great pleasure out of God's word. Let's look at our own lives. What do you take pleasure in? Many things and many people give me a sense of pleasure. I know people that are a delight to be around. I desire to be around them because of it. Also, some activities give me great pleasure. Again, I desire to do them because of the sheer pleasure they bring me.

This woman finds her pleasure in something that we don't think of at first when we think of pleasure. In our secular society, we think of something pleasurable as something that appeals to one of our senses. The blessed woman is first and foremost a spiritual woman and she gets great pleasure from spending time in God's word.

1. "Praise the LORD. Blessed is the man who fears the LORD, who finds great delight in his commands." (Psalm 112:1)

When you read the Bible, do you find delight in it? Does it give you pleasure?
Explain why or why not.

2. "Why spend money on what is not bread, and your labor on what does not satisfy? Listen, listen to me, and eat what is good, and your soul will delight in the richest of fare." (Isaiah 55:2)

What are you spending most of your time and money on? Does it satisfy your soul or do you still feel empty inside? What do you think is the "richest of fare"?

II. "Is in the law of the LORD,"

What? This woman's delight is in the law of the Lord, but how can that be? Isn't the Bible just an old dry book that hardly anyone reads anymore? The law of the Lord is an expression that is used to describe God's word, the Bible. When this psalm was written, the people had what was called the Torah. It was the first five books of the Bible consisting of Genesis, Exodus, Leviticus, Numbers and Deuteronomy. The Priests read it to the people and the people memorized it as a matter of course. It was passed from one generation to another that way.

Today, we have the Bible. It is a collection of sixty-six inspired books. Inspired means God-breathed. Several men wrote these books, but we believe that it was God who inspired the words. That would set this book apart from all others and its words would hold great wisdom and knowledge for all who read it.

Most people own at least one Bible. Several homes have many Bibles. It could be one of the most under-read books around. It may look pretty with a soft leather cover and gold-leaf on the edge of the pages; but if we don't pick it up and read it, we will never discover the wonders that are inside.

3. "I delight in your decrees; I will not neglect your word." (Psalm 119:16)

With our busy schedules and limited time, it is easy to neglect reading the Bible. What part of your schedule can you change so that you can read it on a regular basis?

4. "Your statutes are my delight; they are my counselors." (Psalm 119:24)

When you have a problem or question in your life, do you go to the Bible to find counsel? Would you go there more often if you knew it could really help you?

III.   **"And on his law"**

This woman is reading God's law. She is spending time in the word of God. If we want our lives to be blessed, we need to spend time in the Bible. That pretty book on the book shelf or by our nightstand needs to be opened up and read. It's okay if the pages get dog-eared or if we underline and write in it. It's a book we can and should wear out by reading it regularly.

What is in it that is so great? First of all, if God inspired the words, it just might have some very important things to say to us. Some have called the Bible, God's love letter to man. In it we find great wisdom and learn the story of how God has reached out to his creation, man, in order to redeem him from the power of sin. In the Old Testament, we learn about the beginning of the human race and we see how God chose different people to share his message with. It also gives us a history of the Hebrew people and how God dealt with them and the nation Israel before the time of Christ.

In the New Testament, the first four books are called gospels. In them, we learn about Jesus and what he did and said while he was on the earth. The next books are called epistles or letters, they were written to different churches and individuals. They give us instruction on how to live our lives. Finally, we can read prophecy about the future in the book of Revelation.

Can anyone read this book? I believe so. However, it is easier to understand if you have God's Spirit living inside of you. He will then teach you about it. I tried to read it many times before I was a believer, and I didn't get much out of it. It is a spiritual book and it's contents are best spiritually discerned.

5. "Direct me in the path of your commands, for there I find delight." (Psalm 119:35)

In the first lesson, we talked about a wrong path to walk on. Did you know that God's word provides a path, or way, for you to walk on? How do you think your life would be different if you were to walk on this path?

6. "Let me understand the teaching of your precepts; then I will meditate on your wonders." (Psalm 119:27)

Did you know that we need God's help in order to understand his words? Do you pray for understanding before you read it? Try it and write down the difference it makes.

IV.   "He meditates day and night."

The woman that is blessed by God meditates or thinks about his law day and night. How would a person do that? Well, for starters, let's think about what we do think about day and night. We might think about all kinds of things throughout the day. As women, we may think about what we are going to eat, or cook for dinner. We may think about our children or our relatives and what is going on in their lives. We may think about what we are going to wear. We may think about bills that we have to pay and wonder or worry about where we are going to get the money to pay them. We may watch a lot of television or movies and we may think about what we saw. We may spend a lot of time on the internet and spend a lot of time thinking about what we learned there or who we talked to that day.

Does what we read influence us? As a teenager and an avid reader, I would read some of the popular novels of the day. The characters were very worldly, and were involved in lots of negative situations. They would solve their problems in a very worldly and sometimes unwholesome fashion. I used to think about them a lot, and wanted to be like some of the characters in the novels. Looking back, I can see that those novels had a negative influence on my life and on my perspective.

I have since learned to be very careful about what I read and what I watch on the television. Even though I know lot of it is fictional, it can still influence my way of thinking and speaking. I try to spend my time reading and watching positive things. I also spend time in the most positive book of all, the Bible.

If we want our lives to be blessed, we are going to have to read the Bible and then purposely set our minds on something we read. It may be a verse that speaks to us or one that we want to memorize to help us with something we are going through. If we have read a story about someone in the Bible, we may want to think about their lives and how God helped them deal with the problems they were facing.

The easiest way to do this though, is to find pleasure in what we have read. When you are reading the Bible, and a certain verse jumps out at you, that is God speaking to you. He is trying to talk to you through his word. That should give you great pleasure that he would use his word to communicate something to you personally. Whenever that happens to me, I am encouraged and want to share it with others. Naturally, it is in my mind that day and I think about it. I don't even need to make myself think about it, I just do it because it means something to me.

For years, however, I had problems with meditating on God's word. I would say to myself that I was going to think about it all day, but sure enough, an hour later I was thinking about the usual things I normally think about. Recently, I began to memorize scripture. It wasn't the first time I had done it, but this time because of the effort involved, I would find myself thinking about the words over and over during the day. I would take the card I had written the words on with me wherever I went. I would see it in my wallet or on my desk at work. It was constantly in my mind. It was the first time I could honestly say, I was meditating on God's word during the day.

7. "Oh, how I love your law! I meditate on it all day long." (Psalm 119:97)

If we love something, we think about it a lot. It is only natural. What do you spend most of your time thinking about?

8. "Do not let this Book of the Law depart from your mouth; meditate on it day and night, so that you may be careful to do everything written in it. Then you will be prosperous and successful." (Joshua 1:8)

The Israelites were commanded by Joshua to meditate on God's word day and night. If they did, they would be successful. Can you see how this could be true in your life?

I think that is the real secret of the blessed woman. She is spending time in God's word and God is speaking to her through it. She is finding great pleasure in the communication that is going on between herself and God. How could she not be blessed? The Creator of the universe is speaking to her. Wow, what a thought! No wonder she thinks about it day and night. In the next lesson, we will see what this woman's life looks like when she does this. In the meantime, why not pick a verse of scripture to memorize and try to keep it in your mind this week?

Valerie Cullers

The Psalmist's Tale

David awoke with the first rays of the sun. He had slept well; his dog Hector had only growled a few times during the night. He looked at Hector; he was sleeping for the moment. He remembered the first time he had seen him. He was just a puppy, but was so lively, he had stood out from the rest of the brood. David knew from his breeding that he would make a great dog for sheep herding.

He had wanted to name him Hector, after the traveler who had come through their village when he was a child. The man had been kind and strong, and had told the village children tales of his travels. David thought he was the most courageous man he had ever met, and by far he was the most interesting. He also had a lively sense of humor, and he would give the children riddles to try to solve until he saw them next. Some of them had such a simple solution, and he would laugh exuberantly as he told them the answers.

David liked the name, it was a strong masculine name, even if it was Greek. He would never name a Hebrew child after the man, but he thought he could get away with naming a dog after him. His brothers protested, but since he was the one who would be caring for the puppy, he got his way.

After David had eaten his breakfast, it was time to take the sheep to the streams where they could drink. Most of the year, the streams weren't much to speak of, but during the spring when the rains came, they ran over their banks into the meadows. He had to watch the sheep carefully when the waters were high. One of them could drown if its hooves got caught in the mud. Sheep didn't seem to have the sense to try to get out, they would just stand and bleat until they were too tired to stay upright. David didn't want to be dragging any sheep out of the mud this morning. He didn't want to smell wet wool the rest of the day either.

David started out and Hector got the sheep moving. It wasn't long until David saw the trees. They looked like a dark green oasis at the end of the valley. There were about twenty trees growing in a small area, and water was flowing on the east and west sides of them. David might keep the sheep near there for a while, so he could enjoy the shade they provided. If it were fall, he would enjoy the lush fruit that would hang from their branches, but this time of year there were only leaves.

"A pity," he thought. He always enjoyed eating fresh fruit from those trees. He was still eating the figs his mother had dried in the fall. As he was musing about the fruit, or lack thereof, a thought came to his mind unbidden:

"He is like a tree planted by streams of water, which yields its fruit in season and whose leaf does not wither. Whatever he does prospers."

Of course! That is what the blessed man was like, the one who had been meditating on the law of the Lord. What a great comparison! There was nothing better to this shepherd than streams of water with fruit trees on the banks. What a delight to the eyes and refreshment to the senses they provided. And even when the fruit was not on them, you could always count on the shade they provided. He liked the picture, and this evening by the fire he would work on the melody for this next line.

As for today, he would enjoy the water and the shade as it was going to be another warm day. Beads of sweat were already forming on his forehead as he walked towards the end of the valley.

LESSON THREE

"He is like a tree planted by streams of water, which yields its fruit in season and whose leaf does not wither. Whatever he does prospers." (Psalm 1:3)

This third verse shows us a word picture of what the life of the blessed woman can be compared to. The psalmist had certainly seen lush fruitful trees by streams of water. He probably had known men and women whose lives fit this description, also.

What about us, what and who have we seen that we could compare this word picture to?

I. **"He is like a tree planted by streams of water,"**

Years ago, I remember being at the headwaters of the Klamath River. The river has its beginnings as the outflow of a lake that bears the same name. Downstream, it becomes quite large, flows through two states, and eventually empties into the Pacific Ocean.

At the headwaters, all of the trees that live along its edge are green and strong. The roots run along the banks of the river and they are always well watered. There are some of the most lush fruitful trees around because of their water supply. Drought never affects them because they always get the first of the water as it runs from the lake.

The woman who delights in God's word and meditates on it day and night is like one of those trees. She receives her spiritual nourishment from the word and it becomes a part of her. It is what sustains her and makes her strong.

When we think of a tree, we think of something that has a certain amount of strength to it. Most trees can take many storms and a lot of wind because their roots have grown deep into the ground. They are not easily moved by anything. We want to have that kind of staying power in our lives.

When we plant ourselves in God's word, we will become like those trees. We will develop strength as we spend day after day in the word. Bit by bit, our lives will take on a strength and stability that can come no other way. We will be able to stand firm as the storms of life blow our way. We will have this ability because our roots have grown deep into the word of God.

1. "For the word of God is living and active. Sharper than any double-edged sword, it penetrates even to dividing soul and spirit, joints and marrow; it judges the thoughts and attitudes of the heart." (Hebrews 4:12)

Did you know that God's word has the power to reveal what is really going on inside of you? Can you recall a time when it convicted you of sin and caused a change in your life? Explain.

2. "Let the word of Christ dwell in you richly as you teach and admonish one another with all wisdom, and as you sing psalms, hymns and spiritual songs with gratitude in your hearts to God." (Col. 3:16)

As you read God's word, can you see it working in your life? Do you feel strengthened, nourished or encouraged by it? Give an example.

II.   "Which yields its fruit in season"

As beautiful as most trees are, they do not exist just to be pleasing to our eyes. They have many different functions. This particular tree is productive, it yields its fruit in the season it is supposed to. We want to be like this tree. We want our lives to yield the fruit they should in whatever season of life we are in. What kind of fruit should we produce?

The New Testament talks about two kinds of fruit that our lives should yield. One is produced on the inside and the other is produced on the outside of us. The first one that we will look at is the one developed on the inside of us.

Galatians 5:22-23 says: "But the fruit of the Spirit is love, joy, peace, patience, kindness, goodness, faithfulness, gentleness and self-control. Against such things there is no law." As believers, the Holy Spirit lives inside of us. As we stay planted in God's word, the Holy Spirit works in our lives and produces these different qualities. This does not happen overnight. Just as you see fruit grow on a tree, these qualities are developed over a period of time. They will continue to grow and develop as we nourish ourselves in God's word and stay connected to the Holy Spirit.

Just as a tree develops a certain amount of strength by the storms that it endures, so the fruit in our lives can be developed by the many trials and adversities we face. These challenges give us the chance to rely on the Holy Spirit and let him mold us into the people God created us to be. The world should be able to see a difference in our lives because of where we are planted and what is being produced in us.

The second kind of fruit that will be produced in our lives are good works. These should witness to the work of the Holy Spirit inside of us and produce fruit not only in our lives but in the lives of others also. Ephesians 2:10 says: "For we are God's workmanship, created in Christ Jesus to do good works, which God prepared in advance for us to do." This means that before we were born, God, in his sovereignty, prepared good works for each of us to do. Every day when we wake up, God already has plans for us and things he would like us to accomplish. We need to yield ourselves to him and ask him what he wants us to do. Then we need to be prepared to do them.

The best way to apply this principle to your life is to start your day with prayer and Bible reading. Confess any known sins to God and then ask him to fill you with his Holy Spirit. Ask him to guide and direct you through the day. As you go about the course of your day, be open to any direction you feel he is giving you. You will be surprised to see how he can use you if you are open to his plans and purposes.

The plans he has for you may come in many different forms. They might consist of helping, witnessing, or praying for others. He might want you to share your food or clothing with others. He might want you to baby-sit someone's children or visit an elderly person. These activities, when guided and prompted by the Holy Spirit, will produce eternal fruit in our lives and in the lives of others. We will help facilitate the work of God as he works in and through us.

Many people may not want to hear our words about the Lord or the gospel, but few can fight against or deny the power of loving deeds done in Jesus name. Even the most hardened soul may soften when someone offers to pray for her in a time of crisis. Many discouraged people just need a kind word, and the Lord will prompt us to give one if we are attentive as we go about our daily affairs. His plan is to use us every day in the lives of others in big and small ways.

3. "Remain in me, and I will remain in you. No branch can bear fruit by itself; it must remain in the vine. Neither can you bear fruit unless you remain in me." (John 15: 4)

In order to bear fruit, we must remain in Christ. What specific things are you doing to help you stay close to him?

4. "You did not choose me, but I chose you and appointed you to go and bear fruit – fruit that will last." (John 15:16a)

The Lord has a purpose for your life. He desires that you produce fruit that will last for eternity. What are some things that you are doing to help produce eternal results in another person's life?

III.   "And whose leaf does not wither."

Have you ever seen a well watered garden? Everything is lush and green. The leaves on the plants are not brown or withered. Just as a leaf that is green is constantly getting its nourishment from the plant it is on, so we will be nourished as we meditate on God's word.

God has a limitless supply of nourishment for our souls in his word. As we spend time in it daily, we will have all we need to sustain us for each day. Our spirits will not wither and die like a leaf that has lost its connection with the source of its food supply.

Have you ever seen plants or trees in the middle of the summer when the heat is at its hottest? Only those plants and trees that have an adequate water supply can stand up against the heat of summer. It is the same when a storm comes, those leaves that are green do not get blown off the tree as easily as the brown and withered ones do.

When we spend time in God's word, we become like a tree in a well watered garden.

We will soak up the teaching, wisdom, counsel and knowledge that God has to offer us there. We will get to know him better, and we will develop a strength and understanding that can only come from him.

Not surprisingly, we see a similar passage in Jeremiah 17:7-8: "But blessed is the man who trusts in the Lord, whose confidence is in him. He will be like a tree planted by the water that sends out its roots by the stream. It does not fear when heat comes; its leaves are always green. It has no worries in a year of drought and never fails to bear fruit." I was pleasantly surprised when I saw this parallel passage of scripture. Trusting in God and in his word will yield the very same results in our lives. I don't know about you, but I want to be like a fruitful tree; sharing the nourishment I receive with others and thriving even during the difficult times.

5. "The days of the blameless are known to the Lord, and their inheritance will endure forever. In times of disaster they will not wither; in days of famine they will enjoy plenty." (Psalm 37: 18-19)

Can you think of a time when you experienced disaster and because of the kindness of the Lord you did not wither? Or was there a time of famine when you enjoyed plenty? Describe what happened.

6. "And if you spend yourselves in behalf of the hungry and satisfy the needs of the oppressed, then your light will rise in the darkness, and your night will become like noonday. The Lord will guide you always; he will satisfy your needs in a sun-scorched land and will strengthen your frame. You will be like a well-watered garden, like a spring whose waters never fail." (Isaiah 58: 10-11)

This is a promise for those who follow God's ways and do his will in helping others. Have you ever been rewarded by God when you have helped others?

Write an example from your own experience.

IV. "Whatever he does prospers."

Wow, whatever he does prospers. My dictionary defines whatever as "everything or anything that." [7] In other words, everything that this woman does prospers. In the same dictionary, prosper is defined as "to be fortunate or successful; thrive."[8] So we could use the definitions of these words and paraphrase this line as: Everything or anything that she does is successful and thrives. What a picture! Can you imagine a woman who succeeds in everything she decides to do? When this person looks back on her life, she does not see a series of failures. The things she has set her hand to have been successful and they are thriving.

This picture is of the ideal person. I don't know anyone that has not made mistakes or experienced failure of some sort. I certainly have had my share of failures, and can relate most of them to not taking the time to pray and seek God's guidance from his word.

If we want to spend time meditating on God's word, we will have to be deliberate about it. We will have to choose a verse, passage or story to think about and then begin to ponder it. We can do this as we go about our daily lives, but we may need to tune out some of the noise around us. We may have to turn our televisions, CD players or radios off as we try to do it. Ask God to help you form this new habit in your life.

[7] "He who gets wisdom loves his own soul; he who cherishes understanding prospers." (Proverbs 19:8)

Over and over, the scriptures tie wisdom and understanding to prospering. What can you

---
[7] The American Heritage Dictionary, Second College Edition. Boston, MA: Houghton Mifflin Company, 1976. 1374.
[8] The American Heritage Dictionary, Second College Edition. Boston, MA: Houghton Mifflin Company, 1976. 995.

do in your life to get more wisdom and understanding in a specific area? How would it help you to be more successful in that area?

8. "How sweet are your words to my taste, sweeter than honey to my mouth! I gain understanding from your precepts; therefore I hate every wrong path." (Psalm 119: 103-104)

Ultimately, we make a choice as to the paths we take in life. How will loving the word of God keep you on the right path so that you will prosper in all your ways?

In this lesson, we've looked at what it looks like to be a blessed woman. We've seen her compared to a fruitful tree that is well watered. In the following lesson, we will look at the life of a wicked person, and what God compares her life to. Until then, why not start soaking up the riches that are stored in his word?

The Psalmist's Tale

It had been a good day by the streams of water. A cool breeze had come up in the afternoon and had refreshed him. It was time to take the sheep back to the cave, but before he went, he wanted to walk to the end of the valley and look down on his home in Bethlehem. If he could just see it, he would feel closer to his family and think about the things they would probably be doing this time of day.

He loved the view. The small village of Bethlehem was below with its fields of wheat and barley. He had helped with the harvest before and enjoyed the camaraderie of his brothers as they worked to get the crop in. It was one of the only times they treated him with respect, and when they called to him to help them, they used "little brother" in a favorable way.

Because of his age, he usually got to ride on the sled with a heavier person in order to break up the stalks and loosen the grain from them. That was really fun. When they were finished with that, the winnowers would toss the grain in the air in order to separate it from the chaff. If you were down wind, you would be completely covered with chaff.

As he was thinking about the chaff, and how he had to shake his clothes out to get all of the pieces off, the thought came to him:
"Not so the wicked! They are like chaff that the wind blows away."
He knew the Lord had given him this thought. What a contrast! The blessed man's life was like a lush green fruitful tree but the wicked man's life was just the opposite. It was like the chaff, which had no useful purpose.

The thought gave him pause, and sobered him. He really did fear the Lord, and wanted to please him, but he hadn't thought much about the consequences of not following Him and His law. It almost frightened him when he thought about what had happened to the Egyptians when his people had left Egypt. Their land had been left barren by the plagues God had sent and many of their soldiers had perished in the Red Sea.

Truly, the God they served was awesome and inspiring. He rewarded those who did good and punished those who did evil. He was like a strict loving parent who would not tolerate his children's bad behavior. And who could blame him? He didn't create man to run roughshod over each other, and harm the weak.

As he turned back towards the sheep, he was deep in thought. He wanted his life to count for something. In his heart he was determined to serve the Lord and be the man God had created him to be.

Right now, he was just a young teenager who cared for the sheep. It didn't seem like he would ever get away from them, let alone out of Bethlehem. But he wanted to do something great for God. He wanted to be a righteous man who loved and served the Lord and who made a difference in Israel.

Hector was running ahead of him and was starting to round up the sheep. He realized he was starting to daydream about the future, and that he had better tend to his small flock. It would be easy to leave one behind, if he wasn't paying attention.

LESSON FOUR

**"Not so the wicked! They are like chaff that the wind blows away."
(Psalm 1:4)**

What a contrast! We have just finished a lesson on the benefits of spending time in God's word and how it affects a woman's life. Now, we are going to get a look at what the life is like of a woman who does not follow the Lord or spend time in his word.

I.   **"Not so the wicked!"**

This sentence ends with an explanation point. It is supposed to emphasize the statement. What is the problem with the wicked? Why are their lives not producing good fruit? Psalm 36:1 says: "An oracle is within my heart concerning the sinfulness of the wicked: There is no fear of God before his eyes." In order to begin on the right path in life, we must have a basic fear, or reverence, for God.

Before we can have a basic reverence for God, we must first believe that He exists. I have met many people that do not believe in a personal God. They believe in some kind of a positive force in the universe, but they choose to not believe that there is actually someone who created them and the universe. Hebrews 11:6 says: "And without faith it is impossible to please God, because anyone who comes to him must believe that he exists and that he rewards those who earnestly seek him."

Are you having a hard time with the concept of a personal God? I don't know about you; but I find it hard to believe that the earth and the universe just came into being by chance. For me, it takes more faith to believe that than to believe it was all created by God. Go outside on a clear night and look at the stars. Are you overwhelmed by their beauty and the immensity of the universe? Psalm 19:1 states: "The heavens declare the glory of God; the skies proclaim the work of his hands."

That's who we're talking about here. He is someone who is all-knowing, all-loving, all-powerful and everywhere at the same time. He wants us to acknowledge that he is God and have a reverence towards him.

He also wants us to get to know him by reading his word. Our problem could be the same one that the wicked have. They are not looking in the right place for their wisdom and knowledge. They are seeking their answers from sources other than the Lord and his word.

We usually associate the wicked with what they do, but here we are looking at what they are not doing. Clearly their mind is not tuned to the Creator of the universe. They are not looking to the only One who can give them what they need for a blessed, fruitful life.

1. "The fear of the Lord is pure, enduring forever. The ordinances of the Lord are sure and altogether righteous." (Psalm 19:9)

How would you associate the fear of the Lord with his word?

Does reading God's word cause you to be more reverent towards him?

2. "Humility and the fear of the Lord bring wealth and honor and life. In the paths of the wicked lie thorns and snares, but he who guards his soul stays far from them." (Proverbs 22:4-5)

Why is humility related to the fear of the Lord?

How can you guard your soul from following the paths of the wicked?

II.   **"They are like chaff"**

The next part of this verse shows us what they are like in God's eyes. In our modern culture, we think of the definition of chaff as "trivial or worthless matter."[9] We use this when we talk about something that has no value. When the writer of this psalm used this word, he was talking about the literal definition of chaff: "the husks of grain after separation from the seed."[10]

In Biblical times, the entire process of harvesting, threshing and winnowing grain was done by hand. People knew that after the grain had been harvested, it would be threshed to divide the grain from the husks. These husks were considered worthless. They were not saved for anything.

---

[9] The American Heritage Dictionary, Second College Edition. Boston, MA: Houghton Mifflin Company, 1976.255.

[10] Ibid.,p.255.

When the psalmist describes the wicked like the chaff, he is saying that in the end, their lives will not produce anything of lasting value. To place it in a context we can understand, we may think of someone who has pursued a life of crime. When he looks back at the life he has led, he will see that it has not produced anything positive.

However, all of the wicked do not look like that picture. Some may seem to be very successful. They may have fame and are well thought of by the world. But we must not be taken in by what we see. Psalm 37:1-2 says it this way: "Do not fret because of evil men or be envious of those who do wrong; for like the grass they will soon wither, like green plants they will soon die away." We must not look at them and compare ourselves to them. They may be benefiting from their lifestyle here on earth but will not receive a positive reward in eternity.

Does that exempt us from loving and praying for them? No. We know that God loves all men and sent his Son to die for them. John 3:16 says: "For God so loved the world that he gave his one and only Son, that whoever believes in him shall not perish but have eternal life." If God cares so much for each human being, so should we. We must never regard anyone as worthless, no matter what they do. When they are referred to as chaff, we must think in terms of their ultimate destiny. That should make us even more concerned to pray for and witness to those that God puts in our path.

3. "But I tell you: Love your enemies and pray for those who persecute you, that you may be sons of your Father in heaven." (Matthew 5:44-45a)

Jesus tells us to pray for those who persecute us. The people doing that may seem wicked to us. How well are you able to follow that command?

Can you remember a time when you prayed for someone who was persecuting you and you saw actual changes in your life or in the person's life you were praying for? Explain.

4. "And pray in the Spirit on all occasions with all kinds of prayers and requests. With this in mind, be alert and always keep on praying for all the saints." (Ephesians 6:18)

How is your prayer life? Are you able to pray for others as much or more than you pray for yourself or your own needs?

III.   **"That the wind blows away."**

"After the grain was harvested, it was brought in from the fields and dumped on the threshing floor, a leveled area of hard-packed earth. Oxen dragged sleds, weighted by the driver and perhaps a small passenger or two, over the harvest to loosen the kernels of grain and to break up the stalks. Winnowers then tossed the grain into the air so that the breeze would carry the chaff away."[11] That is the way the process worked in Israel during the time this psalm was written.

Have you ever been working in your yard when a strong wind came up? If you had been weeding and there were little bits of plant on the ground, the wind would have carried them away. Have you ever thought about trying to find all those pieces? No matter how light the wind was, it would be impossible to find each little piece.

That is what this verse is talking about. Ultimately, we will seek the wicked, but not be able to find them. Psalm 37:35-36 describes it this way: "I have seen a wicked and ruthless man flourishing like a green tree in its native soil, but he soon passed away and was no more; though I looked for him, he could not be found." This verse is talking

---
[11] Great People of the Bible and How They Lived. Pleasantville, New York: Reader's Digest, 1974.130.

about finding the man on the earth, but we are talking about finding him in eternity.

The question is, "Who will ultimately be found in the presence of God and who will not?" If we have scorned God and his word our entire life, we cannot hope to be found where he is. If people knew and believed the truth from God's word, they would not want to be lost. They would want to be found in God's presence for all eternity.

Many people believe this life on the earth is all there is. They live with the idea that when they die, that will be the end of their existence. That is not what the Bible teaches. It teaches that there will be an ultimate day of reckoning and there will rewards and punishments handed out. Let us learn to live a life with our ultimate end in mind. It will make a big difference in what we do and the choices we make.

5. "For the Son of Man came to seek and to save what was lost." (Luke 19:10)

Jesus came so that men would not be lost for eternity. Do you have a real concern for the lost? Are you praying for them and witnessing to them when God gives you the opportunity? Can you remember a time when you witnessed to others?

6. "But in keeping with his promise we are looking forward to a new heaven and a new earth, the home of righteousness. So then, dear friends, since you are looking forward to this, make every effort to be found spotless, blameless and at peace with him."
(II Peter 3:13-14)

Are you living your life in light of eternity? Are you making every effort to live a life that is spotless, blameless and at peace with the Lord? What challenges do you have?

We have just finished a lesson of a life compared to chaff. It's not a pretty picture.

Our next lesson will look at what happens after a person dies. Our actions do count for eternity. If you are like me, you want to live your live for the Lord and receive praise from him when that time comes. Let's remember to keep spending time with the Lord in His word. We can't go wrong if we do!

Valerie Cullers

The Psalmist's Tale

David had taken the sheep back in the cave for the night. A small fire was burning and he leaned back on the wall with his harp in his left hand. Tomorrow, he would head back home with the sheep. He would get some more provisions and spend a few nights with his family and sleep in his own bed.

The sheep were resting quietly for the night. They were full of the green grass they had been eating in this fertile valley. At home they would forage in the field at the end of their property and at night they would sleep in the sheepfold.

He sat back thinking about the words the Lord had been giving him. He had been working on the melody this evening. He had also really begun to think about the difference between the righteous and the wicked. For the first time in his life, he seriously meditated on man's ultimate outcome and what would happen to them when they stood before the Lord. That's when the next line in the song came to him:

"Therefore the wicked will not stand in the judgment, nor sinners in the assembly of the righteous." Apparently, God was showing him that there would be two judgments. One for the righteous and one for the wicked. He had never really thought about that before. He thought that there would be just one large gathering of all of the people who had ever lived. There everyone would get their just rewards.

The priests had their own ideas of how everything was going to work out and he had heard a few of them. He was young and had not given them much thought. He was much more interested in growing up and getting to do something else besides guard the sheep all of the time.

Would it ever happen, this great dream of his? He knew that Samuel, the prophet, had anointed him, but he had no idea how his life would turn out and how all of the changes would come to pass. Right now it seemed it would take forever to grow into a man and be someone whom his family respected, let alone someone who would serve God as a leader in Israel.

What deep thoughts he was thinking, and here he was up in the hills outside of Bethlehem. He couldn't be further from the action taking place in Israel. Even now, King Saul's army was pursuing one of their enemies. His father would not even think about letting him enter the army. After all, he was only fourteen and his father would not consider allowing him do anything else until he was at least eighteen years old. It was difficult, but he tried to be content where he was. The only enemies he would get to fight would be the predators that came after the sheep. They weren't the Philistines, but he had taken his sling, and with the Lord's help, had killed a lion and a bear that had tried to take one of the lambs. When he told his father about this, his father had remained thoughtful, but his brothers had laughed at him scornfully. They would never believe he could do anything that showed any kind of strength or bravery. After all, he couldn't beat them in any physical matches.

What could he say? He kept these things and the words the Lord was speaking to him to himself. The only one he might even mention them to was the prophet Samuel and he had only seen him once. He was getting sleepy, someday…someday… he would show his brothers that he really was a man whom they could respect.

LESSON FIVE

"Therefore the wicked will not stand in the judgment, nor sinners in the assembly of the righteous." (Psalm 1:5)

When we read this verse, we are looking at a time in the future. Why would anyone want to stand in the judgment? The whole idea sounds frightening to me, doesn't it to you? What about the assembly of the righteous? That's a different story, we would love to stand there. But where is it going to be, and how will we know that we can be there?

I. **"Therefore the wicked will not stand in the judgment"**

Have you ever been in a court of law? Did you ever get a traffic ticket and had to stand before a judge and get your sentence? I remember being in small claims court where I had to tell a judge how a man had taken my down payment on a rental that did not turn out to be what it had been advertised. I presented my case and the owner presented his. There were a few tense moments while we waited for the judge to make his decision. Fortunately for me, the judge ruled in my favor. The whole experience made me feel afraid, though. I was twenty and the landlord was older and wiser. I didn't know if I had a chance or not, but I had done what people told me to do. I had written down everything that had happened and the order it had happened in. Because I was prepared, the judge could see what the facts were. The landlord just had his word and his testimony was very vague. He wasn't prepared for his day in court and he lost the case.

Each of us will have a day in court with the Judge of the Universe. I'm sure it will be sobering as we see what He will say about the life we lived and what we did with what he gave us. There is a way to be prepared for this day and we will look at how to do this.

In the Bible, two judgments are talked about; the Judgment Seat of Christ and the Great White Throne Judgment. The Judgment Seat of Christ is for those who have accepted Christ as their savior and lived their life for him. The Great White Throne Judgment is for those who have rejected God and his plan for their salvation and have lived their life on their own terms.

The Judgment Seat of Christ is described in 2 Corinthians 5:10: "For we must all appear before the judgment seat of Christ, that each one may receive what is due him for the things done while in the body, whether good or bad." Just as the scripture says, all believers will come before Jesus Christ. The things we have done on earth since we came to know him will be judged.

The things we did before we came to know Christ have already been judged. The Bible says that Jesus took the punishment we deserve when he was on the cross. "He was delivered over to death for our sins and was raised to life for our justification." (Romans 4:25). Because of these words, we know that the sins we committed before we came to Christ are forgiven.

We also know that after we have come to Christ, our sins can be forgiven. We read in 1 John 1:9: "If we confess our sins, he is faithful and just and will forgive us our sins and purify us from all unrighteousness." We should constantly be taking advantage of that promise and confess any known sins that the Holy Spirit brings to our mind.

After we come to Christ, the works we do for him will go through a purifying fire. 1 Corinthians 3:11-15 says: "For no one can lay any foundation other than the one already laid, which is Jesus Christ. If any man builds on this foundation using gold, silver, costly stones, wood, hay or straw, his work will be shown for what it is, because the Day will bring it to light. It will be revealed with fire, and the fire will test the quality of each man's work. If what he has built survives, he will receive his reward. If it is burned up, he will suffer loss; he himself will be saved, but only as one escaping through the flames." As the scripture says, we are to be very careful to build on Christ so that our work will survive the test, and that we will be rewarded for it.

1. "Moreover, the Father judges no one, but has entrusted all judgment to the Son." (John 5:22)

How do you feel about being judged by Jesus? Is he your Lord and Savior or does the idea of being judged by him make you afraid?

2. "Just as man is destined to die once and after that to face judgment." (Hebrews 9:27a)

Have you thought much about facing a judgment after you die, or do you live without thought as to the consequences of your actions?

Do you believe in reincarnation, hoping to get another chance at life in order to correct past mistakes? Can you see that the scripture teaches us that this concept is not true?

3. "So Christ was sacrificed once to take away the sins of many people; and he will appear a second time, not to bear sin, but to bring salvation to those who are waiting for him." (Hebrews 9:27b)

For those who have trusted Christ as Savior, seeing him is something to look forward to. Do you look forward to seeing Christ? Why or why not?

II. The Great White Throne Judgment

This judgment is described in Revelation 20:11-12: "Then I saw a great white throne and him who was seated on it. Earth and sky fled from his presence, and there was no place for them. And I saw the dead, great and small, standing before the throne, and the books were opened. Another book was opened, which is the book of life. The dead were judged according to what they had done as recorded in the books."

At the Great White Throne judgment, the people are judged according to their works, not on the basis of the finished work of Christ. They did not call on Christ to forgive their sins and now their life is being judged according to the good and bad things they have done. Revelation 20:15 says: "If anyone's name was not found written in the book of life, he was thrown into the lake of fire."

How can our names be found in the Book of Life? When we accept Jesus as our Savior, our names are written in the Book of Life. It is a simple process. First, we must acknowledge that we have sinned. The Bible says in Romans 3:23: "For all have sinned and fall short of the glory of God." Everyone, period. No one has lived a life that was up to God's perfect standard. Next, we must repent or turn away from our sins. Acts 2:38 says: "Repent and be baptized, everyone of you, in the name of Jesus Christ for the forgiveness of your sins." Then we must have faith in the Lord Jesus Christ. We must believe that he has the power to save us. It says in John 3:15: "That everyone who believes in him (Jesus Christ) may have eternal life." We must then ask him into our heart; that is called being born again. John 3:3 states: "In reply Jesus declared: I tell you the truth, no one can see the kingdom of God unless he is born again." After we do this, we need to tell others of the decision we have made. Romans 10:9 says: "That if you confess with your mouth, 'Jesus is Lord', and believe in your heart that God raised him from the dead, you will be saved."

It can be as simple as praying a prayer something like this: Dear Jesus: I am sorry for the things I have done and the life I have lived. I desire to turn away from my old way of life. Please cleanse me from my sins and come into my heart. I want to live for you from this day forward. Amen.

God will do the rest. He will give you a new heart and a brand new life. He will guide and direct you through the Holy Spirit who now lives in you. As a Christian, you will need to seek out a local Bible believing church. There you can spend time with other believers and be strengthened in your new life by being taught the word of God. You can get a Bible for yourself, and begin reading it. God can and will change you through the power of the Holy Spirit and his word.

I remember when I made that decision. I was twenty-four years old and had made a a lot of mistakes in my life. My life separated into two categories that day; my life before Christ and my life after I accepted him as Savior. My life began to change as I read from the Bible and the Holy Spirit worked inside of me. I was baptized, joined a church and was taught by godly men and women who knew much more than I did. It has made all the difference in my life and I shudder to think of what my life would be like without the Lord. I hope you have made that decision and are experiencing new life in Christ. It will make all the difference for you, too.

4. "He commanded us to preach to the people and to testify that he is the one whom God appointed as judge of the living and the dead." (Acts 10:42)

Do you think the world knows that they will be judged by Jesus Christ? Is this a truth that you now grasp?

5. "All the prophets testify about him that everyone who believes in him receives forgiveness of sins through his name." (Acts 10:43)

What a choice we must all make: either be judged by our deeds or accept the Lord's forgiveness for our sins while we can. Have you trusted Christ as your Savior? If not what is keeping you from doing so?

III.   **"Nor sinners in the assembly of the righteous."**

We looked at the fact that the wicked will not be at the Judgment Seat of Christ, but now there is another place that we will not find them. They will not be in the assembly of the righteous. Where is the assembly of he righteous and what will they be doing? I believe this verse is talking about a group of people that will be around God's throne worshiping Him. In Revelation 7:9, the apostle John describes a scene he is seeing in heaven. He says: "After this I looked and there before me was a great multitude that no one could count, from every nation, tribe, people and language, standing before the throne and in front of the Lamb. They were wearing white robes and were holding palm branches in their hands. And they cried out in a loud voice: "Salvation belongs to our God, who sits on the throne, and to the Lamb."

This scene is in heaven, but when the Lord comes back to earth to set up his kingdom, there will be people assembled to worship him wherever he is. The scripture says that there will be a new heaven and a new earth and that the Lord will dwell in the New Jerusalem. Revelation 22:3 says: "No longer will there be any curse. The throne of God and of the Lamb will be in the city, and his servants will serve him." I know that I want to be in the assembly of the righteous wherever they are meeting.

We don't have to wait until we are in heaven though to worship the Lord. We have the opportunity in our local churches to worship him and to spend time with other believers. In the New Testament, we are commanded to do this. Hebrews 10:25 tells us: "Let us not give up meeting together, as some are in the habit of doing, but let us encourage one another-and all the more as you see the Day approaching." If we want to stay fervent in our faith, we must spend time with other believers. It is too easy for our faith to become cold or lukewarm when we are not challenged by the teaching and fellowship we get in a local congregation of believers.

My favorite part of church is the worship and praise time. Throughout the week, different songs come into my mind and I find myself humming the songs I heard during the service. If I have been unable to attend church that week, there is a void inside of me. I have missed something that I cannot get on my own. I believe it is the special bond that comes from worshiping the Lord together with a group of believers.

Valerie Cullers

We need to view ourselves as part of a flock who need a shepherd to help guide and protect us. We do have an enemy who would love to destroy us. His name is Satan. If we do not stay with the group, we are easy targets and can get picked off by our adversary. He loves to attack the weak and the disconnected. There is safety in numbers, in nature and in the church. Jesus is speaking in John 10:10: "The thief comes only to steal and kill and destroy; I have come that they may have life, and have it to the full."

The Bible describes the church as the Body of Christ. Christ is the head of the body, and we all compose the different parts of it. 1 Corinthians 12:27 says: "Now you are the body of Christ, and each one of you is a part of it." We all have a part to play in helping Christ's body function the way it was intended to function. Can you imagine how your body would work if your hand or foot decided it didn't feel like doing anything one day? It would make it very hard for you to do anything. It is like that in the church. Each person has something to contribute, and if we don't show up, the church is lacking a vital part of what it needs to operate the way it was designed to.

7. "Praise the LORD. Sing to the LORD a new song, his praise in the assembly of the saints." (Psalm 149:1)

We are commanded in this verse to praise God in the assembly of the righteous. Have you been able to find a church to worship God in? If not, what is stopping you from finding one?

8. "They devoted themselves to the apostles' teaching and to the fellowship, and to the breaking of bread and to prayer." (Acts 2:42)

The early church chose to meet together for many purposes. Have you chosen to meet with a local congregation of believers in order to be strengthened in your faith? Can you name some positive benefits from doing so?

As you can see from the scripture, there are places we want to be and things we want to be doing with the Lord. There are two choices, two roads and two eventual places to spend eternity. Why not make the right choices now so that your future will be secure in the Lord?

Valerie Cullers

The Psalmist's Tale

The sun was just rising in the east. As David stirred, he felt the coolness of the dawn. He looked at the fire and it was a pile of smoldering embers. If he wanted to get warm, he would have to place another few sticks of wood on it to get it burning again.

Today, he and the sheep would walk across the valley and down the hill to his father's house. He was looking forward to seeing everyone and hearing if there had been any news from the battle. He worried about his brothers, just like his father and mother did. He didn't know what he would do if any of them didn't return from battle. He didn't even like to think about the possibility.

"For the Lord watches over the way of the righteous, but he way of the wicked will perish."

The thought came unbidden, but it was such a comfort. Of course, the Lord would watch over his brothers, but those wicked Philistines would perish! They were idol worshipers and were always trying to encroach on Israel's territory. They had no problem cursing the living God, and the thought of it made David's blood boil.

He would use the thought as the last line of the song. It would finish it out perfectly. He might even sing it to his mother if she were having one of her headaches. He hoped she would like it and it would bring her comfort.

He started to gather his things for the walk home. He was looking forward to a real dinner this evening. His cheese and bread could not beat his mother's cooking and he could stand to have a full stomach tonight. His bread was pretty hard this morning and he was already tasting the fresh bread that would be baking in her oven.

It would be a good day, he and Hector would watch the sheep on the way home, but he wouldn't worry about them. The Lord was watching over him, too, and he was sure he was watching over the sheep, also. As he passed the grove of trees, he would be careful, but not afraid of what could be hiding in it.

Yes, it would be good to be home. The sheep would be in the sheepfold for the night and he could rest easy in the house. His own bed was even looking good. A few nights rest would strengthen him for another trek up into the hills next week. He liked going back and forth, because in the summer he would have to go farther to find green grass and he would come home less often.

After a few hours, he was halfway home. One of his dad's servants came up the hill to find him. His dad wanted him to hurry home, because he wanted David to take some cheese and bread to his brothers where they were camped. Eli, his father's servant, would take the sheep the rest of the way home.

David started running. What an exciting adventure, to get to go to the battle and be with his brothers! He could hardly wait to experience the sights and sounds and all of the activity. It was a dream come true! Was there anything better than to be with the men? He might even get to see King Saul. His thoughts were a jumble as he ran down the hill. Could this be the beginning of something new in his life? Only the Lord knew.

LESSON SIX

**"For the LORD watches over the way of the righteous,
but the way of the wicked will perish." (Psalm 1:6)**

We have now come to the last verse in this psalm. Again there is the contrast between the life of the righteous person and the life of the wicked one. There is a sense of finality in the last verse in the psalm. One person will be protected and taken care of because she knows the Lord. The other person will perish, and the work she has done in this life will not last from an eternal standpoint.

I.   "For the LORD watches over the way of the righteous"

The Hebrew word for watches over means "to know"[12] It could be said this way, "For the LORD knows the way of the righteous." Have you ever felt that no one really knew you? Have you ever felt that no one really saw what you did and that your life had little value? We can find comfort in the fact that one Person really does know us and sees what we do. The scripture assures us of these things. In Job 23:10 we find: "But he knows the way that I take; when he has tested me, I will come forth as gold." The same Hebrew word is used here. The writer has a confident knowing that God sees what he does and

---

[12] Strong, James, <u>Strong's Exhaustive Concordance of the Bible</u>. (A Concise Dictionary of the words in the Hebrew Bible) Hendrickson Publishers. P.18.

will eventually reward him for the things he has done.

Before I was a believer, I didn't really find comfort in the fact that God saw everything I was doing. Many times, I felt guilty before him, and I didn't have any confidence that my sins had been forgiven. I didn't know that he really loved me and that he had been watching over me from the moment I was born.

In Jeremiah 1:5 we read: "Before I formed you in the womb I knew you." God knew you in the womb, formed you and is watching over you now. The Lord has a plan for your life, and you need to seek him in order to find it. Jeremiah 29:11 says: "For I know the plans I have for you," declares the LORD, "plans to prosper you and not to harm you, plans to give you hope and a future." We need to diligently seek after the Lord to find out what he would have us do with our lives. When we do that, we will have the confidence that we are doing what he created us to do, and we will be able to live a life that pleases God.

1. "All the ways of the LORD are loving and faithful for those who keep the demands of his covenant." (Psalm 25:10)

Do you find this verse to be a comfort in your life? Why or why not?

2. "Those who know your name will trust in you, for you, LORD, have never forsaken those who seek you." (Psalm 9:10)

Can you see the importance of not only God knowing you – but you knowing God? Explain the benefit in this verse.

Have you experienced this in your own life? Share an experience.

If you are thinking that it is too late for you, you are wrong. You may have lived a self-centered life, not thinking of anyone or anything besides yourself. But just the fact that you are doing this study shows that you are interested in something different. It is never too late to turn to the Lord and begin again. He is always waiting to bring you back to himself. Over and over in the Bible the Lord calls people to repent and to turn back to him. In Hosea 2:23, the Lord says: "I will say to those called 'Not my people' 'You are my people'; and they will say, 'You are my God.' " God is just waiting to begin a personal relationship with you or renew a relationship that has grown cold.

Perhaps you knew the Lord previously, but you have wandered far away from him. You know he knows your life, and that is what you are worried about. Come back to him. He loves you more than you could ever imagine, and he is waiting to offer you forgiveness and restoration. In Luke Chapter 15, there is a story about a young man who left his father's house and squandered his life and resources away in loose living. When he gets sick of the life he is living, he comes to himself and decides to return to his father's house. He doesn't know what to expect from his father. What he doesn't know is that his father has been longing for him to return home. When his father sees him, he runs to greet him. He holds a celebration dinner for him, to show him that he has been forgiven and restored to the family.

More than any other, that story portrays the heart of God the Father for his children. He wants us to be restored to him and be in right relationship with him. Then, we can lead the kind of life he wants us to lead and we can fulfill the plans he has made for us.

Maybe you are not living a life in open rebellion to the Lord, but your heart is far from him. You knew him once, but you no longer have a vital relationship with him. You go to church every Sunday, but you are just going through the motions. You have let your relationship with him grow cold through neglect. He is waiting for you to return to him and he will rekindle that relationship with you. When we feel far away from God, it is usually because we have turned away from him. He doesn't turn away from us.

3. "If we claim to be without sin, we deceive ourselves and the truth is not in us." (I John 1:8)

Are you thinking that there is no hope for you? Do you feel that you are a sinner and that other people don't struggle with sin the way that you do? What does this verse say about that?

4. "If we confess our sins, he is faithful and just and will forgive us our sins and purify us from all unrighteousness." (I John 1:9)

Would you like to take this time and confess anything to God that is keeping you from a right relationship with him? Write your prayer to him.

II. "But the way of the wicked will perish."

One of the definitions for way in my dictionary is "a course of conduct or action."[13]

We understand that this verse is talking about the lifestyle of a wicked person. His way

---

[13] The American Heritage Dictionary, Second College Edition. Boston, MA: Houghton Mifflin Company, 1976. 1368.

will perish. The things he has done while on earth will not have any lasting value. They will literally perish. In Proverbs 14:12 we read: "There is a way that seems right to a man, but in the end it leads to death." It is very easy to live a life and use yourself and your ideas as the standard for right and wrong. It takes deliberate thinking to seek out truth beyond yourself and your present concepts of right and wrong. A person has to be willing to confront truth in light of the scriptures in order to see his real state.

Many know right from wrong and are making a deliberate choice to do wrong. In Romans 1:30 we read the phrase: "they invent ways of doing evil." God is speaking of depraved people that are consciously choosing to do wrong. They are even inventing ways of doing evil. The way of that person is going to perish. She will not leave anything of eternal value behind her. She will also not take anything of eternal value into eternity.

I don't know about you, but I want my life to count for something. When I die, I want to know that I have done something positive with my life. I want it to count in an eternal sense. My desire is to be used by the Lord to help bring others to himself. People will live forever in one place or another and I want to help people spend eternity with the Lord. Sometimes, that means saying no to some activities that in themselves are not bad, but are very time consuming.

My life is similar to that of many women; I have a job, a family, a house to clean, laundry and shopping to do. I have a limited amount of free time, so I have to be careful with the commitments I make for that time. I have to pray and evaluate what organizations, if any, I will be involved in. There are requirements and responsibilities that go with joining any group, so I have to really think about what would be the best use of my time from an eternal perspective. Over the years, I have passed up joining many worthwhile organizations that do a lot of good work, but I have no regrets.

When I was in my thirties and forties with children at home, I felt I could only add one activity to my schedule. I chose to lead a Bible Study at my church. When I look back at that choice, I am satisfied that my time went for something that may have brought something of eternal value to the lives of others. Each of us has to pray and ask the Lord what he would have us do with the limited time he has given us.

5. "Do you not know that the wicked will not inherit the kingdom of God?"
(I Corinthians 6:9a)

Have you settled in your heart that there is not a positive eternal reward for wickedness or are you still tempted to view wickedness as something to be desired for the temporary satisfaction it brings?

6. "Do I take pleasure in the death of the wicked? declares the Sovereign LORD. Rather am I not pleased when they turn from their ways and live?" (Ezekiel 18:23)

How would you describe God's heart as it is described in this verse? Does it surprise you that God takes no pleasure in the death of the wicked?

You don't have to be wicked or evil to be following your own way, though. In Isaiah 53:6 we read: "We all, like sheep, have gone astray, each of us has turned to his own way." It is the natural response of man to go his own way and do his own thing. It takes an intervention from God in our lives to turn us to the correct way. Not one of us stands guiltless before a holy God.

The solution for the wicked, as it is for all of us, is to turn to God. Isaiah 55:7 says:

"Let the wicked forsake his way and the evil man his thoughts. Let him turn to the LORD and he will have mercy on him, and to our God for he will freely pardon." God is and has the only way out of our dilemma. In John 14:6, Jesus says, "I am the way and the truth and the life. No one comes to the Father except through me." God, through his Son Jesus, has provided us with a way out of our problem and a way into his life, which is eternal life.

Even after we come to the Lord, we can't live a sinless life. In James 3:2 we read, "We all stumble in many ways," and we do. We make mistakes but we can always be forgiven if we take our sinful thoughts and actions and confess them to God. We can never be perfect, but we don't have to be. There was only one perfect man, and that was Jesus Christ. The rest of us need to seek to obey God and his word. Then we can have confidence that our loving Heavenly Father will reward our efforts when our time on earth is ended.

7. "However, to the man who does not work but trusts God who justifies the wicked, his faith is credited as righteousness." (Romans 4:5)

Have you placed your faith in God and his son Jesus Christ? If so, what makes God see you as righteous?

8. "For the grace of God that brings salvation has appeared to all men. It teaches us to say "No" to ungodliness and worldly passions, and to live self-controlled, upright and godly lives in this present age, while we wait for the blessed hope – the glorious appearing of our great God and Savior, Jesus Christ, who gave himself for us to redeem us from all wickedness and to purify for himself a people that are his very own, eager to do what is good." (Titus 2:11-14)

According to this verse, what has Jesus done and what is he doing for you?

What kind of life do you want to be leading when he appears? Are you leading that kind of life now? Is there anything you need to change in order to be leading a righteous life?

As we conclude our study of Psalm One, my hope is that you have a better perspective of your life in light of eternity. My prayer for you is stated in Colossians 1:10: "And we pray this in order that you may live a life worthy of the Lord and may please him in every way; bearing fruit in every good work, growing in the knowledge of God."

May you continue to learn and grow in Jesus Christ and in his word, the Bible. You will be assured of a fruitful life and have many rewards in eternity. May you always live a blessed life!

Psalm One for Women on the Run

LIGHTHOUSE PUBLISHING 2013